The Scientist's
Guide to Physics™

Discovering
Quantum
Mechanics

GINA HAGLER

ROSEN
PUBLISHING®

New York

Published in 2015 by The Rosen Publishing Group, Inc.
29 East 21st Street, New York, NY 10010

Library of Congress Cataloging-in-Publication Data

Hagler, Gina, author.
Discovering quantum mechanics/Gina Hagler.—First
edition.
        pages cm.—(The scientist's guide to physics)
Includes bibliographical references and index.
Audience: Grades 7–12.
ISBN 978-1-4777-8002-2 (library bound)
1. Quantum theory—Juvenile literature. I. Title.
QC174.123.H34 2015
530.12—dc23
                                                  2014009060

On the cover: a quantum wave
Manufactured in China

Contents

INTRODUCTION

Physics is the branch of science that concerns itself with matter, energy, and the ways in which they interact. Scientists in this discipline strive to explain the way the universe works. Beginning in the 1600s, physicists busied themselves with questions about the observable world. Why do the planets orbit the sun? Why is the sky blue? Why are some objects attracted to magnets? Why does a compass point to the north? Why do apples fall from trees? All of these are questions that can be answered and explained with the theories of what is known as classical physics—the physics of what we can observe with the naked eye.

By the end of the nineteenth century, physicists had developed working theories to explain forces and motion; the temperature of objects; and the relationship between electricity, magnetism, and light. They were confident that the few remaining questions of the day would soon be answered. Albert Einstein reinforced this confidence when he added his theory of special relativity to the existing body of knowledge in 1905. His theory extended classical physics to answer some nagging questions related to the Newtonian theory of gravity.

In 1900, German physicist Max Planck set out to answer a simple question related to lightbulbs. He had no idea his work would open the door to a new branch of physics. He only wanted a better understanding of the relationship between heat and light. The question was straightforward. The answer would open the door to a whole new field of physics.

The problem was that the physics of Planck's time—classical physics—described light as a wave. No matter how Planck looked at it, the results he obtained were not consistent with this description. Frustrated with his inability to solve the problem, he decided to work backward. In doing so, he discovered his observations could only be explained if light energy traveled in packets: quanta. Planck theorized that each of these quanta was made up of a specific

amount of energy. When he treated light energy in this way, rather than as a wave, he not only obtained the results he needed, he also obtained results that made sense when used in other observations.

Planck could not have realized it at the time, but with his use of quanta, he had taken the first step into a new type of physics: quantum physics (also known as quantum mechanics). While classical physics provided explanations for the observable world, quantum physics provided explanations for the subatomic world. It would be used to explain the behavior of matter and energy in the world of the very small and the very fast, the world where a microscope was a necessity. The results and explanations provided by quantum physics would not always seem logical, but they were amazingly accurate. Because of this, it would not be long until quantum physics was looked to as the discipline for providing the explanations that classical physics could not.

With the introduction of the quanta, Max Planck opened the door to an entirely new branch of physics.

CLASSICAL PHYSICS

Chapter

1

A t the end of the nineteenth century, classical physicists could look back on the accumulated knowledge gained during three hundred years of scientific investigation into the workings of the observable universe. They had solid explanations for force and motion, known as mechanics; heat and entropy, known as thermodynamics; and electricity and magnetism, known as electromagnetism. They could trace theories from

Sir Isaac Newton created the laws of motion.

QUESTIONS OF THE DAY

By the end of the nineteenth century, classical physicists had done an excellent job of explaining most of the readily observable behavior of the universe. Classical physics provided an explanation for why apples fell, why bridges stood, why magnets lifted needles, why grass was green, and why skies were blue. Classical physicists were certain they would soon have the answer to the few questions that remained:

1. The Ultraviolet Catastrophe. Classical physics predicted that a blackbody—one that consumed fuel while allowing no energy to escape from within—would emit radiation of infinite power. If this happened, a furnace or coal stove would, theoretically, emit radiation that reduced anything or anyone nearby to ash. Clearly this was not the case. What could explain this phenomenon?

2. The Photoelectric Effect. In classical physics, light travels in a wave. That theory provided an acceptable explanation of the way light traveled from one place to another. The problem was, when an electric current in a metal sheet was exposed to light, the energy of the electrons that were emitted did not vary with the intensity of the light. It was also discovered that at some intensities, there was no effect at all. How could this be?

3. The Nature of Light. Did light move in a wave or as a particle? Was it possible that it moved as one or the other depending on the circumstances? Classical physicists had not expected to see the narrow frequency ranges that formed the lines in a spectrum. What did this mean about the nature of light?

4. Structure of the Atom. The atom had been imagined as everything from a solid substance to a plum pudding. Did atoms exist? If so, were they truly indivisible or were there particles that made up the atom?

their origins, through their different iterations, and on to their current forms. With all of this in hand, it was difficult for them to imagine that there could be anything that classical physics would not soon explain. In fact, it was widely thought that there was very little left to discover.

Of course, classical physicists did not know they were classical physicists. To them, they were scientists, perhaps physicists, who were seeking explanations about the workings of the world that were visible to the naked eye. What made color? Why did things fall? Why did the planets stay in orbit? These were huge questions of the time—and each received thorough treatment that resulted in a satisfactory explanation.

Mechanics

Classical mechanics, also known as Newtonian mechanics, provided explanations for the motion of objects that are larger than microscopic and move at speeds that are slower than the speed of light. Mechanics deals with mechanical energy. This energy is made up of two types of energy. One type is potential energy that exists in the form of the energy stored in an object. This energy depends on the position and shape of an object. The other type is kinetic energy, in the form of the energy an object has because of its motion.

Sir Isaac Newton created three laws to describe mechanics. His laws, based on the work of those who came before him, became the definitive laws for problems concerned with forces and motion.

Newton's first law of motion states that an object at rest remains at rest unless acted upon by an unbalanced force. An object in motion remains in motion unless acted upon by an unbalanced force.

This law deals with inertia. You know from experience that a baseball sitting on the ground remains in that position until something acts as a force upon it, such as if someone picks it up or the wind blows and moves it. You also know that you can expect an object moving through a frictionless medium to continue forever in the same direction without stopping.

The player with the ball would remain in motion if not acted upon by the player attempting to make the tackle.

Newton's second law of motion states that a force or forces acting upon an object will accelerate that object in the direction of the net force.

This law deals with momentum. How fast and how far an object acted upon moves depends on the net force and the mass of the object. You know from experience that it takes a lot more force to move a car than it takes to move a soccer ball. You also know you can "aim" your kick to get the soccer ball to move in the direction

When air is released from a balloon, the balloon moves in the opposite direction from the force of the released air.

you wish. How close the object comes to your target will depend on the net effect of all the forces at work.

Newton's third law of motion states that for every action, there is an equal but opposite reaction.

This law deals with states of equilibrium. You've seen for yourself that buildings will stand for years. This is true because the forces in the structure are in balance.

THERMODYNAMICS

The term "thermodynamics" translates to "heat in motion." It is the branch of science that defines the way heat, work, temperature, and energy relate. The first known speculation about the relationship of heat and work occurred in 1798, when a British military engineer named Sir Benjamin Thompson noticed that heat generated by an activity

is proportional to the work—energy that is transferred through force to another object—being done. This became the foundation for thermodynamics. In 1842, another early theorist, Sadi Carnot, proposed the existence of a heat-energy cycle. Toward the end of

SCIENTIFIC DISCOVERY

It's easy to think that each branch of science is separate from the rest. After all, you learn about chemistry in one class, physics in another, earth science in yet another . . . It's difficult to see what they all have in common until you stop to consider that each of these fields is made up of theories and conclusions drawn by those who have worked hard to explain the world around them. At some level, the material covered in each field relates to the behavior of the same group of objects.

In the same way that the different branches of science overlap in some instances and build on one another in others, the branches of physics continue to evolve and build on one another. At first, there was classical physics. This branch of physics dealt with things in the world that were visible to the naked eye. Quantum mechanics came next. It deals with the physics of the subatomic world.

Particle physics is a branch of physics that studies the ever-smaller pieces of matter that scientists have discovered. At the same time, there are scientists who are working to create a theory of everything—a theory that unites the behavior of matter from the infinitesimally small to the grandest, largest, and most cumbersome.

The more you know about science, the more you'll understand the way the world works. That understanding will serve as a useful basis for the questions you'll come up

with on your own. There's no reason to believe, as the classical physicists did at the end of the nineteenth century, that we are nearly done discovering new things and everything will soon be explained.

that century, Rudolf Clausius introduced two laws of thermodynamics. There are currently four laws of thermodynamics.

The zeroth law of thermodynamics states that when two systems are in equilibrium with a third system, the two systems are in equilibrium with each other.

The first law of thermodynamics states that the energy in a system is equal to the heat added from its surroundings and work done by the system on its surroundings.

This is also known as the law of conservation of energy. You know from your experience that objects near a source of heat can be warmed by the source of heat.

The second law of thermodynamics states that the heat energy per unit temperature in a closed system reaches a maximum level at which no energy is available to do useful work.

It isn't that systems lose or gain heat; it is that they use all available energy.

The third law of thermodynamics states that the entropy [disorder] of a perfect crystal—a crystal in which there is only one structure repeated over and over without imperfections of any kind—of an element tends to zero as the temperature approaches absolute zero, the temperature at which all motion ceases.

This state of energy is the most stable form of the element, since there is the least movement at a molecular level. This point can be used to determine the absolute scale for entropy, which can then be used to determine disorder in other systems.

ELECTROMAGNETISM

Electromagnetism deals with energy that travels in waves. Sunlight is a form of electromagnetic energy. The waves in sunlight have some properties that are electrical and some that are magnetic in nature. Microwaves, X-rays, radio waves, ultraviolet radiation, and infrared radiation are also forms of electromagnetic energy. Visible light and gamma rays are forms of electromagnetic energy, too.

James Clerk Maxwell deduced the equations that meshed light and wave phenomena into

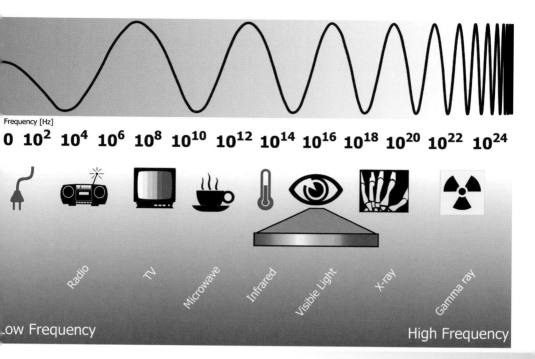

Frequency [Hz]

0 10^2 10^4 10^6 10^8 10^{10} 10^{12} 10^{14} 10^{16} 10^{18} 10^{20} 10^{22} 10^{24}

Radio   TV   Microwave   Infrared   Visible Light   X-ray   Gamma ray

Low Frequency   High Frequency

The electromagnetic spectrum includes a range of wavelengths and frequencies.

electromagnetism. His work showed that electric and magnetic fields traveled together through space as waves. As they traveled, they would switch back and forth, or oscillate, allowing each to have the necessary energy required for its continued existence.

According to Maxwell, all electromagnetic waves are massless and travel at the same velocity. What is that velocity? The speed of light, or about 186,000 miles (300,000 kilometers) per second. The only difference in

the various types of electromagnetic waves is their frequency—the rate at which their electric and magnetic
fields oscillate.

The work done in these three key areas con-
stituted the accepted definition of the way things
worked at the end of the 1900s. It's easy to see why
scientists at the time were so certain they could find
solutions to the few puzzles that remained. They
had no way of knowing that the theories they used
to explain the workings of the visible world around
them would not be the theories that explained the
workings of the subatomic world.

BLACKBODY RADIATION

Chapter 2

W hen scientists study a phenomenon, they strive to eliminate all possible variables that are not related directly to the problem at hand. To do this, they want to be as specific and focused as possible. To help with this, they often imagine an ideal environment for their experiments. This ideal environment does not actually exist in the real world, but if it did, it would allow scientists to test just one aspect of a particular problem.

At the end of the 1800s, one such problem that interested scientists was the question of why an iron rod changed color and glowed as it heated. They wondered if it had something to do with the amount of heat or type of light. They wanted to know so that they could set standards for the new electrical industry. The problem also captured the interest of scientists because it was an interesting thermodynamic question.

To study the light and heat—forms of radiated energy—experienced by the iron rod, scientists had to consider what it would take to create conditions in which all the energy in the system was accounted for. They theorized about an ideal blackbody: a structure that would not allow any of the radiation energy inside of it to escape. This would force the energy inside the cavity of the blackbody to be emitted and reabsorbed over and over again.

Scientists could specify a closed system when they did their calculations. If you were to imagine what such a system might look like in real life, one of the closest ways to envision such a blackbody is to imagine a kiln with iron walls. A kiln is designed to reach and maintain very high temperatures for prolonged periods of time. If you could see inside this ideal kiln through an insulated window, you would see the walls of the interior change color in a particular sequence as the temperature grew higher and higher. The walls might

Imagine this kiln with iron walls that would glow as the kiln grew hot.

This iron rod is different colors because the sections are different temperatures.

even glow—emit visible light—if the temperature were hot enough.

A kiln is a good real-world example of a closed system because there is nowhere for the energy to go. The walls are insulated to keep the heat inside the cavity of the kiln. You could attest to the fact that no energy escaped the kiln if the outer surface of the kiln remained cool to the touch. If the kiln you used were truly lined with iron, your observations would allow you to confirm what scientists had theorized about the original blackbody: an iron rod.

The theory of the iron rod was that it began with a black color and, over time as it was heated, changed in color to glow red and finally white before ultimately cooling down to resume its original status. Scientists wondered if all objects went through the same progression. Did all objects heat and

then cool? How exactly did thermodynamics explain the behavior of blackbodies? The quest for the answers to these questions led to the first realization that classical physics could not explain all of the phenomena at work in the universe.

That was not all. At the time, scientists did not imagine that the answers to their questions about blackbody radiation would one day be helpful to astrophysicists.

INITIAL EXPERIMENTATION

Scientists investigating blackbody radiation hypothesized that a blackbody would emit radiation at all frequencies. Two scientists working independently of one another pointed out some flaws with this theory. The chief flaw was that if a blackbody truly could emit radiation at all frequencies, it would be more likely to emit radiation at higher frequencies than lower frequencies because there were more frequencies between a given frequency and infinity than between a given frequency and zero.

Balfour Stewart, a Scottish scientist, was the first to make significant discoveries with blackbody systems. In 1858, he learned that blackbodies radiate and absorb energy of the same wavelength. Gustav Kirchhoff, a German physicist, confirmed these findings in 1860. In 1896, German physicist Wilhelm Wien developed a formula that allowed him to plot a curve that matched the data from his experiments. The only problem was that, while it matched precisely at short wavelengths, it didn't agree with the data at the longer wavelengths.

Wien wasn't the only one tackling this problem at the end of the nineteenth century. English physicist Lord Rayleigh also created a formula to calculate the curve of heated objects. His curve worked extremely well for the longer wavelengths. It did not accurately portray the curves at shorter wavelengths. Worse still, his formula predicted that the thermal radiation (heat) emitted by a blackbody should increase in intensity at the shorter wavelengths. In fact, it predicted that it could shoot up to infinity at the ultraviolet end of the light spectrum. This prediction was the basis of the ultraviolet catastrophe.

Wilhelm Wien found that his data from longer wavelengths did not match his expectations.

THE ULTRAVIOLET CATASTROPHE

It's rare that you can point to one event and say with certainty, "This was the start." In the case of the ultraviolet catastrophe, it is possible to a large degree. At the start of the 1900s, thermodynamic theory described energy as a flow between radiation and material substances. This flow was unbroken. On the other hand, there were those who believed matter was not a wave at all. They believed it was made up of individual particles known as atoms. You could use their mechanical motions to calculate the thermodynamic properties of a substance.

Max Planck was a well-respected German physicist. He wanted to prove that mechanics and thermodynamics shared common ground. To do this, he performed a series of experiments on a blackbody. He was certain that the energy in a closed system was made up of continuous waves that oscillated within the cavity, in keeping with Maxwell's theory and the second law of thermodynamics.

Cavity—blackbody—radiation had been studied before. It was known that objects being heated would increase in heat and then glow. The glow was light that was being emitted. The color of the light changed with the temperature. Planck made his studies and discovered that light did not behave as a wave at ultraviolet frequencies. The theories predicted that the heat at these frequencies should continue to grow infinitely, reducing everything around it to burned ash. This was clearly not the case. The fact that ultraviolet light did not behave as predicted by the laws of classical physics was, however, a catastrophe; it was the first time a natural phenomena could not be explained by the classical physics of the day. To solve this problem, Planck described light energy in terms of packets called quanta. Each quanta held a specific amount of energy. For Planck, the quanta had relevance only when combined with his constant and applied to problems of blackbody radiation.

Max Planck

Max Planck was a German physicist who had done a great deal of work in thermodynamics. He was interested in the blackbody problem because he wanted to determine the theoretical framework of Wien's work. It was at first inconceivable to him that Wien's formula did not hold true for both large and small wavelengths. He held this view because he was convinced that matter was continuous; there were no smaller building blocks to matter. If you could cut

WHO IS MAX PLANCK?

Max Planck (1858–1947) was a German physicist who was told at the start of his career that there was nothing left to be accomplished in physics; the work was nearly complete. Fortunately for the rest of us, Planck did not listen to this advice because his interest was not in finding new things. He wanted to understand the existing fundamentals. Ironically, in doing so, he went on to identify quanta and usher in an entirely new branch of physics.

Planck's main interest was in the field of thermodynamics. He wanted to understand how heat and energy influenced each other in matter. The focus of his interest was on the nature of radiation from hot materials. It was for his work in blackbody radiation and his theory of the quanta that Planck received the Nobel Prize for Physics in 1918.

As is true of all scientists, Planck had other interests. Before he became focused on mathematics as a child, he had been an excellent musician. He was married and had children. One of his sons died during World War I. During World War II, Planck opposed Adolf Hitler and the Nazi regime. He was openly supportive of Albert Einstein—who was Jewish—and his work. Planck even met with Hitler to try to get him to stop discriminating against Jews. When Hitler paid no attention to him, Planck protested by resigning his position as head of the Kaiser Wilhelm Institute.

After the war, Planck was re-appointed head and the institute was renamed the Max Planck Institute. The Max Planck Society is still in existence today. Seventeen of its research scientists have been named Nobel Laureates. Scientists at the institute continue Planck's legacy of scientific investigation.

an object into ever-smaller pieces, Planck believed, the pieces would not be atoms that were capable of combining in an endless number of ways. You would find that you were creating ever-smaller pieces of the substance being divided. The smallest of pieces would still hold the properties and essence of the whole object.

Planck was familiar with the work of Ludwig Boltzmann. This Austrian physicist focused on the mathematical properties of large numbers of particles in a system—a view of the universe that was the opposite of Planck's. Planck was determined to resolve the problems with the predicted graphs of blackbody radiation while staying true to his belief in the continuous nature of matter. Ultimately, he was not able to do this. The only way to reconcile the discrepancies and create graphs that worked at both short and long wavelengths was to adopt a view of energy that corresponded with Boltzmann's view.

PLANCK AND THE QUANTA

Planck tried repeatedly to create a working formula, based on his view of matter, which would reconcile the work of Wien and Rayleigh and result in a functional theory of entropy in a thermodynamic system. Ultimately, he abandoned this approach to the problem. Instead, he started with what he observed and worked backward through the variables he could control and observe. That left only a question about the nature of the energy itself. Planck determined that energy could not be coming in a steady flow. It must instead exist in the form of quanta—packets of energy that traveled in set amounts. Planck did not envision the quanta as a universal attribute. He viewed energy in this way purely for the purposes of his work with blackbodies. Whatever his reasoning, Planck created a formula that worked at both ends of the light spectrum. Little did he know that he had also paved the way for quantum mechanics.

THE PHOTOELECTRIC EFFECT

Chapter

3

I n 1887, German physicist Heinrich Hertz discovered an interesting phenomenon. He was performing additional work on James Clerk Maxwell's electromagnetic theory of light and, during his experiments, observed sparks being discharged when an electromagnetic wave was detected. With his attention focused on a different problem, Hertz did nothing more than report on his findings. He did not take the time to pursue the cause of these sparks or try to discover what their presence might mean. Given that he was interested in a different set of problems, it's quite likely that he did not realize the significance of what he had observed.

Heinrich Hertz observed sparks being discharged during his work but did not investigate them.

German physicist Albert Einstein, on the other hand, wondered about the meaning of Hertz's observations. He saw the possibilities for additional investigation into the sparks. In the same way that Max Planck had been fascinated by the theoretical problems associated with blackbody radiation, Einstein found himself intrigued by Hertz's discoveries. Perhaps this occurrence was the opportunity to determine the nature of light.

ENTER ALBERT EINSTEIN

Einstein wanted to know more about this photoelectric effect. He wanted to use it to prove that light was either a wave or a particle. To test his theories, Einstein designed a simple experiment in which an

ENERGY AND FREQUENCY

Sometimes people speak about energy. Other times people speak about wavelengths and frequency. Still other times it seems people are saying that energy, wavelengths, and frequency are all related. Is there a relationship between energy, wavelength, and frequency? If there is, what is it?

Energy is the capacity for work. It can be in the form of power or heat. It can be measured for a specific unit or for an entire system. A pulley system uses energy to lift a heavy crate. A piece of wood releases energy when it is burned.

Energy makes its way from one place to another in the form of a wave. A wave can be described as having a long or short wavelength. The wavelength is measured from the top of one wave to the top of another, or from the bottom of one wave to the bottom of another. The more energy is being transferred, the shorter the wavelength.

Frequency is a measure of how quickly a wave vibrates—how large or small the wavelength may be. The faster a wave vibrates—moves up and down—the higher the frequency. The smaller the wavelength—the length between the crest or troughs of a wave—the higher the frequency. If a wave has a large wavelength, it will have a lower frequency.

What does this have to do with energy?

(continued on the next page)

ENERGY AND FREQUENCY

(continued from the previous page)

The greater the energy, the smaller the wavelength and the greater the frequency. The smaller the energy, the greater the wavelength and the lower the frequency will be. This matters when we look at the properties of electromagnetic radiation where wavelengths are related to temperature. As you might guess, the hotter objects have shorter wavelengths, while cooler objects have longer wavelengths. Of course, it's all relative.

electron would complete a circuit upon release. The circuit he created used two sheets of metal as the end points. These sheets of metal were parallel but separated by a space. This space was the distance the electron must cross to complete the circuit. He would shoot light at the metal sheet that stood in as the negative end. It would strike the sheet at an angle. When an electron was released, it would travel across the open space and strike the other metal sheet. Upon contact, the circuit would be complete for an instant.

Einstein theorized that if the light acted as a wave when it struck the metal, it would take some period of time before electrons would be dislodged and complete the circuit. This would be the case because the nature of waves would make it impossible for an electron to be released immediately. If the light acted as a particle when it struck the metal, the discharge of the electron would be immediate.

He also theorized, in accordance with classical physics, that the greater the intensity, the more electrons would be liberated, and the greater the resulting charge in the circuit. To increase the intensity of the light striking the metal plate, he would release a rapid stream of light. If he wanted to vary the energy in the light itself, he would vary the color of the light, since different colors of light are the result of differing wavelengths. Einstein could vary one or the other of these variables to note the effect on the electrons. He would be watching to see how often, how quickly, and under what conditions an electron was freed with sufficient energy to cross the gap, strike the facing metal sheet, and complete the circuit.

EINSTEIN'S RESULTS

Einstein quickly found that electrons were not always released when the light hit the metal sheet. When electrons were released, he noted that they were released immediately upon the arrival of the light

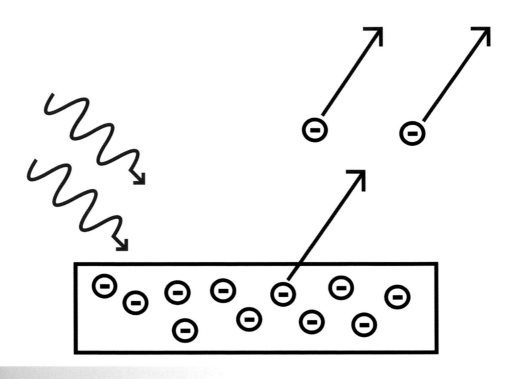

Einstein realized that an electron would be released
only when the stop velocity was exceeded.

on the metal sheet. This was an indicator that light
moved as a particle, but Einstein wanted to address
other questions as well. To do this, he would vary his
other inputs to obtain the information he needed to
answer all the questions that arose about the behavior
of the electrons.

He tried several approaches to determine the reason that an electron was not released every time light
struck the metal sheet. He shot more and more light

at the metal sheet to increase the intensity of the light striking the metal sheet. This did not result in more electrons escaping their bonds, so Einstein varied the wavelength of the light. When he did this, he found that more electrons were released at shorter wavelengths than at longer wavelengths. This was valuable information about the nature of light, but it still did not explain why there were times when the light striking the metal sheet produced no action by an electron.

Einstein deduced that there was some minimum amount of energy that was required to free an electron from its atomic orbit. He theorized that once this velocity was exceeded, an electron would be released. If that stop velocity were not exceeded, the electron would sit tight. Since increasing the intensity of the light had not had an effect on the release of electrons, he decided to use light of different wavelengths. He was able to prove that a blue light (short wavelength) carried more energy than a red light (long wavelength). A graph of this behavior resulted in a straight line, but instead of extending from the origin, it touched the x-axis at a point to the right of zero. This point was the stop velocity.

As Einstein worked, he realized that Planck's constant and his quanta played a part in his calculations. Not only was the energy quantized, but Planck had also been correct in calculating the constant that reflected this reality.

EINSTEIN'S ANNUS MIRABILIS

Albert Einstein is one of the most famous scientists of all time. His work in physics was instrumental to the principles we use today. He developed the general theory of relativity, and his work on the photoelectric effect won him a Nobel Prize for Physics in 1921.

The year 1905 was Einstein's annus mirabilis—his year of wonders. During that year, he published four important papers, plus his doctoral dissertation. The papers he published covered the photoelectric effect with the use of the quantum hypothesis of Planck, the movement of small particles suspended in stationary liquids, the electrodynamics of moving bodies, and the question of whether or not the inertia of a body depends on its energy content. Einstein had not yet found a teaching position, so during that same time he worked as a clerk in the Patent Office.

Einstein eventually held a number of prestigious positions, including the directorship of the Kaiser Wilhelm Physical Institute. He fled Nazi Germany for the United States in 1933. His work was used in the development of the atomic bomb, although he was not a part of the taskforce that produced the bomb. After World War II, he was offered the presidency of the State of Israel, which he declined.

It is said that Einstein viewed problems and advances in science in steps. He understood that his work would form the basis for those who followed, just as those who came before him provided a basis for his own work. With that as his guide, he worked on problems of interest to him in the field of physics until the end of his life.

Einstein was quite famous in his day. When he appeared in public, he was recognized by the general public and treated as a sort of celebrity. When not out in public, he played the violin for relaxation and pondered the complexities of his current projects.

LIGHT AS PARTICLE

Einstein had now demonstrated that light was not a wave. He had proven definitively that light was a particle. His results could not be explained in any other way. He called his quantized light a photon. It was a massless particle that traveled at the speed of light. His work with the photoelectric effect put the photon on the scientific map as a particle that had energy that varied with the wavelength. This was known because not all photons were capable of freeing an electron. The energy of light was dependent on the frequency of that light.

Max Planck (*left*) introduced the concept of quanta. Albert Einstein (*right*) used the quanta to discover the photon.

This helped explain the ways in which matter and radiation could reach thermal equilibrium.

An important distinction between the work of Einstein and Planck was that, while Planck had concluded that light energy was delivered in quanta, Einstein had proven that light itself is quantized. Since Einstein's observations could not be explained within the theories of classical physics, they provided another form of support for the quantum mechanical view of the world.

For Einstein this phenomenon—the photoelectric effect—made it clear that Planck had identified a property when he defined the quanta for use in his work with blackbody radiation. Planck had assumed quanta were applicable to blackbodies only. Einstein theorized that all energy might exist in the form of quanta. If this were the case, then light was not a wave but a particle. While Planck had been the first to introduce the concept of packets of energy, Einstein's work had taken the quanta one step further and resulted in the discovery of the photon.

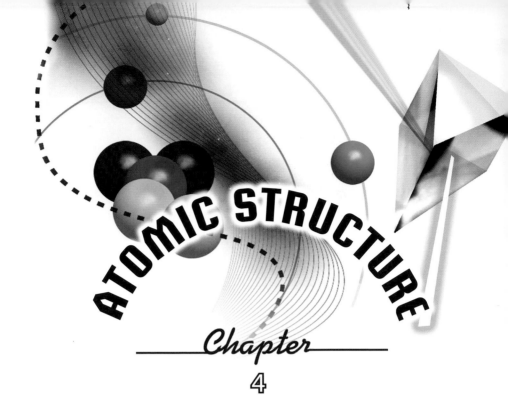

ATOMIC STRUCTURE

Chapter 4

Questions about the composition of matter have been around since at least the time of the ancient Greeks. In fact, it was in 450 BCE that an ancient Greek named Democritus, continuing the work done by fellow Greek Leucippus, first put forth a theory of matter that introduced the atom. According to this theory, everything was composed of particles that could not be divided, had empty space between them, moved constantly, and could not be destroyed. He also concluded that there were an infinite variety and number of atoms. In keeping with his vision of these mysterious building blocks, Democritus called them *atomos*—Greek for "uncuttable."

His theory held until 1661, when Irish scientist Robert Boyle decided that matter was made up of corpuscles—tiny pieces of matter that were independent of one another. Isaac Newton liked that concept

so much, he used it in his definitions of light. It would be another 140 years before scientists created experiments that would prove or disprove these theories through direct observation. Once they did, their observations often fell short of their expectations. We now know that this was because these scientists were taking their first steps into the world of quantum physics.

In 450 BCE, ancient Greek scientist Democritus speculated that atoms—*atomos*—existed.

THE 1800s

In the 1800s, several more scientists would try their hand at theories of atomic structure. In 1803, English chemist John Dalton introduced the law of multiple proportions. The basis of his law rested upon the concept that elements could combine in only specific ways to make up the substances around us. For instance, table salt (NaCl) could consist of one, and only one, part sodium combined with one, and only one, part chlorine. Combine the sodium and chlorine in a different ratio, and you would create an entirely different type of salt. However, it would have traits in common with table salt.

This thinking led Russian chemist Dmitri Ivanovich Mendeleyev to introduce the periodic table in 1869. The periodic table was a very important step in understanding the nature of the world because it showed the ways in which some types of elements had attributes in common, while others simply did not. His work enabled him to correct some properties of elements that had already been discovered, while predicting the properties of elements that had not yet been discovered.

By 1888, Swedish physicist Johannes Rydberg noticed that the emissions from hydrogen contained gaps, or dark areas. In contrast, the spectrum of visible light from an incandescent source showed a continuous spectrum of colors. There were no dark lines; all of the colors were represented. What's more, the spectrum for an element was the same for each sample of that element. To explain the line spectra of hydrogen, Rydberg devised a constant. This constant accounted for the fact that some of an electron had to be free to be part of the spectrum. It also had to have reached its quantum number in order for it to escape the material that held it.

British physicist J. J. Thomson was interested in the behavior of atoms in large electric fields. In 1897, he used a cathode ray tube—a tube in which the atoms were ionized—for his work. Because the atoms were ionized, the electrons inside the tube were free. They did not require anything specific to release them from their bonds. Thomson theorized that the rays in the cathode ray tube were actually made up of a stream of negatively charged particles.

Structure of the Atom

Thomson's Model of the Atom

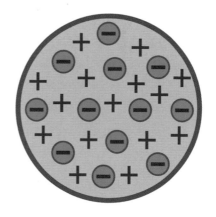

J. J. Thomson created the plum pudding model of the atom.

ATOMIC MODELS, FUNDAMENTAL PARTICLES, AND QUARKS

Each model of the atom built on the work that had been done since the last model. For this reason, the focus of each model differs from the others in an important way.

In 1897, J. J. Thomson proposed a model of the atom that was known as the plum pudding model because it showed negatively charged electrons surrounded by a positively charged "pudding." The focus of this model was on the electron. The problem with this model was that alpha rays could not always penetrate an atom during experimentation. This should not have been the case if Thomson's model was correct.

In 1909, Ernest Rutherford proposed a model of the atom known as the planetary model. In this model, the focus was on the nucleus of the atom. The planetary model showed a positive nucleus with negatively charged electrons around it. The problem with this model was that the electrons should have lost their energy and spiraled inward. This was not the case.

Niels Bohr suggested the solar system model of the atom in 1913. In this model, the focus is on the quantized orbit of the electrons. This model has a small nucleus with a positive charge. The negatively charged electrons orbit this nucleus in rings that are spaced around the nucleus. The problem with this model is that it perfectly explained only the hydrogen and helium atom.

In 1927, Erwin Schrödinger put forth the current model of the atom: the electron cloud model. In this model, the focus is on the fact that the model is not of a definite size. It has negatively charged electrons rotating around the nucleus, as did Bohr's model. The difference is that Bohr's model envisioned fixed orbits, whereas the electron cloud model states that we cannot know the exact location of an electron.

As quantum theory has progressed, so has our knowledge about the fundamental particles—the particles we currently believe are the smallest building blocks—that comprise the atom. So what makes up what?

- Atoms are made up of a nucleus and electrons.
- Electrons are an elemental particle—they are not made up of anything else.
- The nucleus of an atom is made up of protons and neutrons.
- Protons are made up of quarks.
- Neutrons are made up of quarks.
- Quarks are an elemental particle—they are not made up of anything else.

But that's not all. Just because quarks are not made up of anything else does not mean there is only one type of quark! Scientists theorize there are actually six types of quarks. They have some interesting properties and can carry a fractional electric charge. They are also spoken about in pairs. Don't be surprised if you hear about up and down quarks, charm and strange quarks, and top and bottom quarks.

He was able to demonstrate that this was true. He called these particles electrons.

Thomson used his discovery to create a model of the atom. He assumed an atom must have a neutral charge. Because of this, the model he created placed the electrons in a "pudding" of material that held a positive charge. His model is known as the plum pudding model.

Modern Atomic Theory

The discovery of the electron brought atomic theory to an entirely new level. At last there was proof that something existed within matter, even if we could not see it directly. With the plum pudding model as a first approximation, other scientists went to work on their theories.

In 1909, Rutherford, in conjunction with work done by German physicist Hans Geiger and New Zealand physicist Sir Ernest Marsden, performed experiments to further explore the structure of the atom. In their work, they shot alpha particles at a sheet of gold foil. Most of the alpha particles passed right through, but some bounced back. They posited that this was because they were hitting something that was solid. Rutherford called this the nucleus of the atom and

Ernest Rutherford (*left*) and Hans Geiger (*right*) performed experiments that led to the theory that an atom had a nucleus.

based his planetary model on his theory that electrons orbited the nucleus in much the same way as the planets orbit the sun.

By 1913, Bohr created a new model for the atom. It was based on his work with hydrogen and worked perfectly for that element. It would not work with many other elements, but it did present the idea of electrons in quantized orbits. A quantized orbit meant that the electrons could only orbit in distinct distances

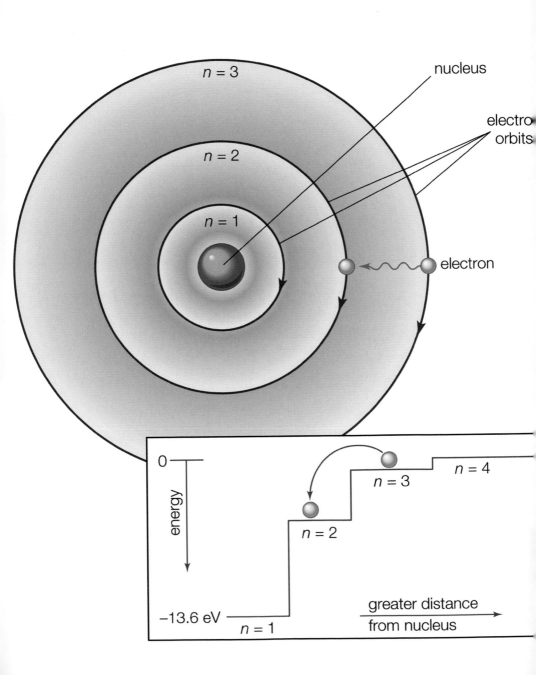

from the nucleus. The distances were dependent on the composition of the particular atom. This model is known as the solar system model.

In 1924, French physicist Louis de Broglie presented a theory of electrons as waves. He suggested that not only electrons but all matter has wave properties. This concept of wave-particle duality was an important step in the development of quantum theory. It led to additional work by German physicist Werner Heisenberg. Heisenberg developed a theory that is fundamental to quantum physics. Known as the uncertainty principle, it states that we can either know with precision the position or the momentum of a particle. Once we determine one, we lose the ability to precisely measure the other. Heisenberg developed this theory in 1927.

Working independently of Heisenberg, Schrödinger came to a similar conclusion that same year. His work led him to a new model of the atom. This is the current model of the atom, known as the orbital or electron cloud model. It does not assume an atom and its electrons take up a specific size each time. It assumes the nucleus and its electrons can take up more or less space as appropriate.

Pictured here is Bohr's solar system model of the atom.

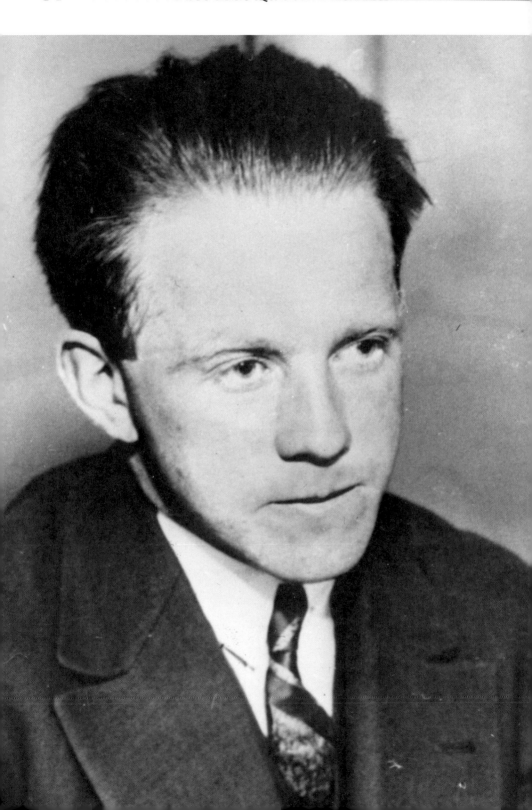

The work done with the atomic models has been important to our understanding of quantum physics. As our vision of the atom becomes clearer, we are able to turn our focus onto the ever-smaller particles we have discovered within the particles that make up the nucleus of the atom. All of this work has been integral to our understanding of the interaction of matter and energy at the subatomic level.

Werner Heisenberg concluded that we can know the position of a particle or the momentum of a particle, but not both.

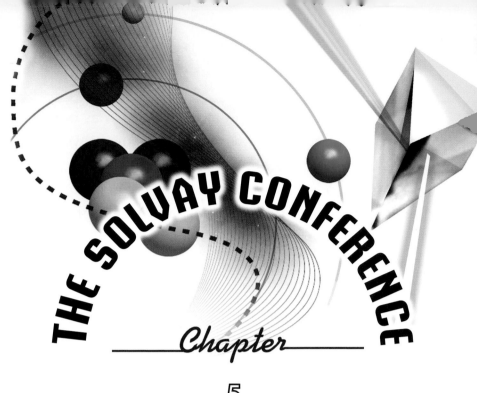

THE SOLVAY CONFERENCE

Chapter

5

I n 1912, Ernest Solvay founded the International Solvay Institutes for Physics and Chemistry to solve pressing problems in physics and chemistry. The meetings are held in Brussels, Belgium. Those who attend must be invited. The conferences are held once every three years or so. Problems related to quantum physics have dominated the agenda since the start.

The Solvay Conference of 1927—also referred to as the Fifth Solvay Conference—was especially important. Many of the scientists in attendance would go on to do the seminal work in quantum physics. Nine of those in attendance were theoretical physicists who had done essential work in quantum mechanics and would receive Nobel Prizes for their work.

The official topic of the conference was "Electrons and Photons." As you can imagine, with a group of such experienced and respected scientists, there was much discussion and disagreement about the new field known as quantum physics.

DIFFERING VIEWS

Planck attended the Fifth Solvay Conference. He was the one who had formulated the idea that energy traveled in packets known as quanta. He had thought his quanta had application to blackbody radiation alone, but since the time of his work, he had come to see that it had a much larger application. Many of the scientists with him at Solvay had taken his quanta, along with the factor he'd developed, and gone on to investigate new phenomena.

Einstein had taken Planck's quanta to the next level with his work on the photoelectric effect by demonstrating that all light is quantized. He'd also already developed his general theory of relativity. He had continued to work on problems related to physics, but that didn't mean he was happy about the move to a new form of physics. He especially felt the idea of superposition—that something could exist in two states at one time—was ludicrous. In arguing the concept with

Bohr, he was reported to have said that God doesn't play dice—meaning that something was one thing or another. It would be several years before he would develop his special theory of relativity that envisioned gravity as a surface, rather than a sort of force field.

The Fifth Solvay Physics Conference was attended by some of the greatest scientists of the time.

Bohr, creator of the solar system model of the atom, was a proponent of quantum theory. His explanation of superposition had satisfied many of the physicists at the conference. The notable exception was Einstein. They would have a running battle on the topic until Einstein's death in 1955.

Heisenberg, author of the uncertainty principle, was in attendance. His theory was new, but it clearly stated that the very act of observing an object at the subatomic level alters the reality being observed. This happened because the measuring device emitted particles of its own, which then interacted with the particles being observed. It made it impossible to accurately measure more than one property of a particle at a time. Because of this, Heisenberg concluded that you could work with only probability and mathematical formulas. (Schrödinger

DOUBLE-SLIT EXPERIMENT

In 1801, English scientist Thomas Young devised an experiment to test the nature of light. The purpose of his experiment was to define the nature of light. The experiment was relatively simple. He would have a boxlike structure with a board with two parallel slits in it at one end, and a blank but solid wall at the other end. He would then shine monochromatic light at the board with the two slits. Because these slits were the only openings in the board, the light could pass through only one or the other of these two slits. If light were a particle, it could only shine on the back wall directly in line with the two slits.

Young performed his experiment and found that light did not appear in only two places on the wall behind the openings. In fact, the light appeared in bands of light and dark along the entire back wall of the box. This made no sense if light were a particle. It made sense only if light were a wave. This was the case because a light wave would be forced to split as it encountered the board with the slits. One part of the wave would pass through one slit. Another

light sou

Thomas Young used a box with two slits for light to enter to prove that light was a wave.

part of the wave would pass through the other. This would result in two waves on the far side of the board. The waves would interfere with each other as they traveled to the back wall of the box. Where the waves matched each other in amplitude, there would be a bright bar of light. Where the peak of one wave matched the trough of another, there would be no light.

Young's dual-slit experiment proved that light was a wave.

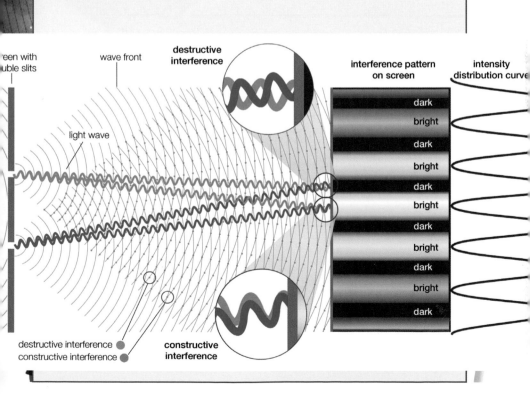

screen with double slits   wave front   destructive interference   interference pattern on screen   intensity distribution curve

light wave

dark
bright
dark
bright
dark
bright
dark
bright
dark
bright
dark

destructive interference ●
constructive interference ●   constructive interference

had reached a similar conclusion with his wave theory.) Bohr struggled with Heisenberg's theory until he concluded that there could be a dual nature to a particle. However, it would only be possible to observe and measure one aspect of the particle. Ultimately, Heisenberg

Erwin Schrödinger, creator of the electron cloud model of the atom, also derived a formula that became the basis for wave mechanics.

and Bohr had developed theories that were compatible. Together their theories, known as the Copenhagen interpretation, formed the foundation for quantum theory.

De Broglie presented a paper at the Solvay Conference. His paper was about the possible dual nature of light. In taking this position, he considered the results of Einstein's work with the photoelectric effect. It was not lost on him that in that context, light had behaved as a particle, while in the double-slit experiment, light had displayed the properties of a wave. De Broglie not only agreed with Einstein's concept of the wave/particle duality of light—the notion that light had properties of both particles and waves—but also carried it a step further. He said it was the motion of a wave that was associated with the motion of a particular particle of any sort. Most of the scientists were

SCHRÖDINGER'S CAT

Is it possible for a cat in a box full of potential poison to be both dead and alive at the same time? It can if it's Schrödinger's cat. To be more precise, the cat can be both alive and dead at the same time if it's a quantum cat. To understand how, we need to take a closer look at the thought experiment on superposition proposed in 1935 by Erwin Schrödinger.

Frustrated that scientists were using his wave function formula in ways he had not intended, Schrödinger proposed he would put a live cat into a steel box. He'd also put a vial of deadly acid, as well as a radioactive substance, in the box. If a single atom of the radioactive substance decayed while the box was closed, a mechanism would trigger a hammer that broke open the vial. The acid would kill the cat. We could not know what had happened inside the box until we opened the box.

Most of us are fine with this line of reasoning until we get to the part where Schrödinger says the cat will be both alive and dead until we open the box. This is because the very act of observing changes the state of what is being observed: the cat cannot remain in a superposition of states once we open the box and learn its condition.

This is one of those puzzles that is at the heart of quantum physics. We know in our everyday lives that something cannot be in one state and in another, although you might argue that something could be in a state of transition. We also know that in the subatomic world of quantum physics, it is possible for something to be in multiple locations, or states, simultaneously.

Schrödinger created this puzzle about a cat to illustrate the absurdity of quantum reasoning in application to our everyday world. Give it some thought and see if you can make sense of it.

unimpressed. After all, they knew from Thomson's work that an electron was a particle. They were not about to consider the possibility of a particle being a wave and a particle. Einstein agreed with de Broglie's work. Both were proven right when de Broglie's theories were confirmed.

Schrödinger came to the conference with a new formula. His formula was based on de Broglie's wave work. He believed his formula represented all forms of energy within a physical system and could be used to represent the underlying quantization of atomic systems. Part of his formula made use of the work with functions done by French mathematician Jean Baptiste Joseph Fourier. Schrödinger's formula for the calculation for the wave function of the system called for the identification of the wave functions of the individual states. By making use of Fourier's Eigen value functions, Schrödinger was able to deal with the problems of the atomic structure of matter. His formula became the basis for wave mechanics.

EFFECT ON QUANTUM PHYSICS

The 1927 Solvay Conference had a profound effect on the field of quantum physics. By selecting a topic in advance and inviting those who were the most respected in their field, Solvay ensured that the papers presented would address the most pressing problems of the time. The discussion generated by those papers, as well as by debate between scientists who were already familiar with the work of their fellow participants, made it possible for quantum theory to benefit from the input of the greatest minds engaged in creating and testing that theory. The fact that the scientists came from throughout Europe, came prepared to debate and discuss their work and the work of others, and were in a position to formulate new ideas as they participated was of monumental importance.

Some of the discussions led to longstanding disagreements of the sort held by Einstein and Bohr. Some of the discussions led to collaboration at best, or the free exchange of ideas at least, between theorists at work on problems based on a similar approach. By bringing these visionaries together, Solvay most certainly helped advance the state of quantum physics and theory more quickly than would have been otherwise possible.

FAST-FORWARD TO NANOPARTICLES

Chapter 6

When we speak about quantum physics, we speak about the ways in which matter and energy interact at the subatomic scale. The surprise for classical physicists has been the science that works so well to explain the workings of the readily visible universe is not the science that works at this very small scale. Nanoparticles are such small-scale, subatomic particles. They are at the heart of the field of nanotechnology. Dedicated to the study and manipulation of structures at the nano (10^{-9}) level, this field focuses on the ways in which particles of a substance behave differently at the nanoscale than at larger scales. Theories of quantum physics can be used to predict and explain the behavior of these particles, but there is more. With these differences in behavior comes a range of potential uses for these materials. These uses range from medical treatments to electronics.

NANO TIMELINE

Work at the nano scale is work at the subatomic scale. Before this work could be undertaken, scientists had to have a way to see these tiny bits of matter. In 1931, German scientists Ernst Ruska and Max Knoll built the first transmission electron microscope (TEM). The TEM could magnify objects by a factor of up to one million. With this microscope, it was finally possible to see things at the molecular level. The TEM was used to study proteins in the human body, as well as metals. It could view particles at this very small scale because it focused a beam of electrons on an object. The electrons then passed through the object, giving a view that was not possible by merely focusing light on and magnifying an object.

The field of nanotechnology received a great deal of attention in 1959, when American theoretical physicist Richard Feynman gave his seminal talk, "There's Plenty of Room at the Bottom," at

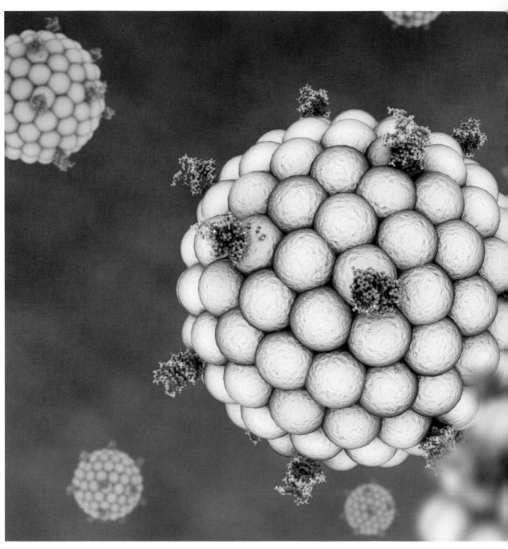

CalTech. Feynman spoke about the potential of nanoparticles. He asked the audience to think about what would be possible if they could manipulate individual atoms—arrange them as they liked. He encouraged them to imagine a world where things could be not just miniature versions

In this image, molecules are embedded in the surfaces of nanoparticles.

of themselves. He encouraged his audience to imagine a world in which things could be built at the subatomic level. In the future, Feynman envisioned, "all of the information that man has carefully accumulated in all the books in the world can be written . . . in a cube of material on two-hundredth of an inch wide—which is the barest piece of dust that can be made out by the human eye."

By the 1970s, scientists were working to create technology for space colonies. This technology would incorporate nanotechnology to allow the components to be orders of magnitude smaller than had ever before been envisioned. In 1974, Tokyo Science University professor Norio Taniguchi used the term "nano-technology" in a paper. According to Taniguchi's definition, nanotechnology would be a

HOW SMALL IS SMALL?

Quantum mechanics is concerned with the behavior of matter at a very small scale. Ping-Pong balls, marbles, rubber bands on your braces, the width of a piece of hair, an individual cell—all of these are small. In fact, lots of things are small. When we talk about quantum mechanics, it would be helpful to know just how small "small" is.

This number line from MathisFun.com shows the relative size of a number of objects. It uses scientific notation for values on the line, which are measured in meters:

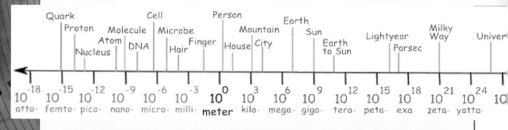

You can see that a person is slightly greater than 10^0 meters in height. This makes sense, since a meter is equivalent to 3.28 feet and 3.28' × 10^0 = 3.28' × 1 = 3.28 feet or 1 meter. A person is generally about 5 or 6 feet, or a bit more than 3.28 feet in terms of this number line. You can also see that the height of a mountain is at the 10^3 mark, or 3.28' × (10 × 10 × 10) = 3.28' × 1000 = 3,280 feet or nearly 1 kilometer. This makes sense when you examine the height of mountains around the world and discover they range up from 2,000 feet.

Find "molecule" on the number line. It appears at 10^{-9} or .000000328 meters in size. This size, 10^{-9}, is also known as a nanometer. Numbers from this size down on the number line are at the nanoscale. The sun is at 10^9 meters in size. This is $3.28' \times 1,000,000,000 = 3,280,000,000$ feet or 3.28 gigameters. If an object as large as the sun (3,280,000,000 feet in size) appears large to us when it is nearly 93 million miles away, imagine just how tiny something as small as a quark must be!

manufacturing process where materials were built by atoms or molecules.

The scanning tunneling microscope (STM) was invented in the 1980s. This new microscope led to the discovery of many new, tiny structures. Dr. Eric Drexler's work, *Engines of Creation*, was published in 1986. In this work, Drexler used the term "nanotechnology" in speaking about molecular nanotechnology. He included the positive and negative possibilities of a technology with the ability to manipulate the structure of matter.

The U.S. National Nanotechnology Initiative was founded in 2000. It exists to coordinate nanotech research and development at the federal level.

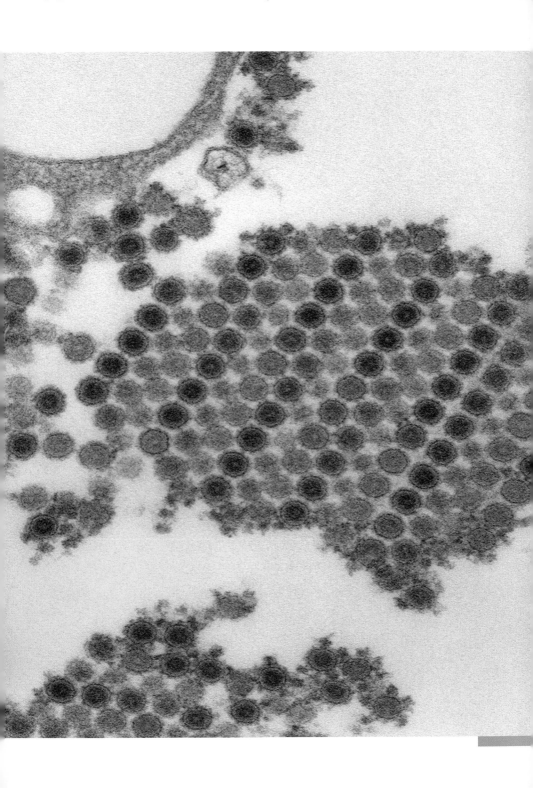

NECESSARY TOOLS

Interest in nanoparticles and nanotechnology is strong for good reason. Scientists have not only discovered that nanoscale materials can occur naturally. They have also moved past simply observing matter at the molecular level to directly manipulating that matter. Now that they can do this, they also have the ability to create nanoscale materials to meet specific purposes. To work at this small scale, specialized tools and technology, such as electron microscopes, are musts. Three of these electron microscopes are the scanning electron microscope (SEM), the transmission electron microscope (TEM), and the atomic force microscope (AFM).

The SEM is used with metals. If a material isn't metallic, scientists coat it with gold. When viewed through the SEM, it is possible to get an accurate image at sizes as small as a few nanometers. When it's necessary to obtain a closer look, the TEM is more appropriate. With the TEM, electrons pass through a very thin sample of an object. Because it takes a long time to prepare a

Here, a virus is viewed through a TEM.

nm

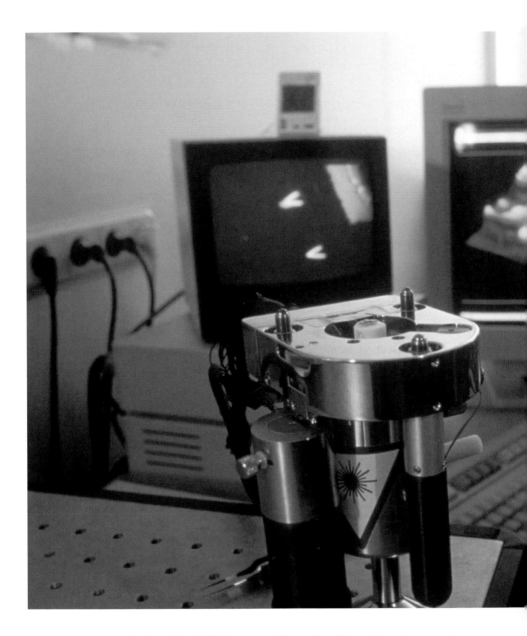

sample for the TEM, as well as the fact that it requires large quantities of energy, the TEM is used only when it's essential to obtain a view with a resolution

This scientist uses an STM to observe the structure of DNA.

of a few tenths of a nanometer. The AFM gives a clear image of a sample's surface. It uses a laser to scan the surface, resulting in an image with the detail of a topographic map.

Observing the nanoparticles is not enough. The actual subatomic matter has to be moved to create a nanoscale material. To help with this, scientists use the STM (scanning tunneling microscope). This type of microscope creates an image in the same way as the AFM. The tip of its probe can also be used to pass an electrical current to a sample. This is an important feature because it reduces the distance between the probe and the sample. To understand how this probe can be used to move atoms, it's useful to imagine a magnet picking up slivers of iron. As the STM moves, the atoms nearest the charged atom move with that charged atom. As with the magnet, these atoms

POTENTIAL OF NANOTECHNOLOGY

Many industries hope to benefit from the use of nanotechnology. The use of nano materials to construct nanoscale components that are both lighter in weight and stronger than the materials available today is of great interest to the auto industry. In the space industry, advances in nanotechnology could lead to materials that can be used to coat the components of space vehicles. These coatings would enhance performance while lightening the load that will be carried into space, thereby reducing the fuel requirement. Nanomaterials also hold promise for other aspects of space travel and exploration; astronauts and others working in space must make their way around in bulky suits. If nano materials could be used to create more forgiving fabrics with the same protection, that would make a tremendous difference to those who wear them.

Governments and universities worldwide are keeping close watch on developments in nanotechnology. They hope to use nanotechnology to solve pressing problems, such as air and water pollution. One application being developed would clean up oil spills before they can spread and cause an irreversible loss of marine life and habitat.

Energy production and efficiency is another area of interest. If nanostructures could be designed to allow some types of atoms to pass through a material while others were not able to, it might be possible to create a process that captured only what was needed to create energy without any waste materials that required disposal. This would also result in more efficient systems that required little maintenance.

For researchers with an interest in the application of nanotechnology, commercialization of their findings is a priority. Commercialization in the form of licenses and permissions make it possible for findings from universities and centers to be used in business ventures. A portion of the earnings is returned to the researcher to pay for additional research.

can be moved to the desired location. This process is called quantum mechanical tunneling.

POTENTIAL USES

The promise of nanoparticles is not limited to the creation of new materials. There is also reason to believe that nanoparticles will play a role in the delivery of medication to tumors and other growths—benign or malignant—within the human body. With this ability,

highly toxic chemotherapy drugs will be able to reach their target without avoidable damage to other tissue along the way. Another possibility is medical testing that can be performed with the reaction of the nanoparticles used as the indicator for the test result. Smart materials created of nanomaterials may someday be used to test the pollution levels of rivers and streams. They may also be used to warn of impending problems in nuclear facilities. Researchers are also excited at the possibility of computers built with components at a nanoscale. Such computers will be constructed at such a small scale that the limitations imposed by larger scale—components that run too hot—can easily be overcome. In this way, tremendous technological gains will be made.

This nanomaterial has been developed to detect cancer. The color of the material that "sticks" to the cancer cell alerts medical professionals that cancer has been detected—and where.

FUNDAMENTAL PARTICLES

Chapter 7

The search is on for fundamental particles. Also known as elementary particles, they are believed to be indivisible pieces of matter. Some of them may prove to be no larger than a single, infinitesimally small point, rather than something comprised of many points. We just don't know yet. Why bother searching for these tiniest building blocks? Their identification will enable us to understand the workings of the world around us at both the visible and subatomic levels.

PARTICLES

Scientists have actually been thinking about or searching for fundamental particles since the time of the ancient Greeks. Today, we know that the atom is not indivisible; it's made up of a nucleus and electrons. We also know that while the electron is indivisible, the nucleus is made up of protons and neutrons. Those, in turn, are made up of quarks. Quarks are fundamental particles. This means they are not made up of anything smaller. At least they're not made up of anything smaller that we know about at the moment. Scientists have designed a classification system to keep track of these tiny building blocks.

PARTICLE CLASSIFICATION

The elementary particles are known as quarks and leptons. (These particles make up non-fundamental particles known as fermions.) There are six "flavors" of quarks. The six "flavors" are broken into pairs known as up and down; charm and strange; and top and bottom. These quarks can be combined to form other particles, but since those particles are made up of quarks, those other particles are not fundamental

STANDARD MODEL OF ELEMENTARY PARTICLES

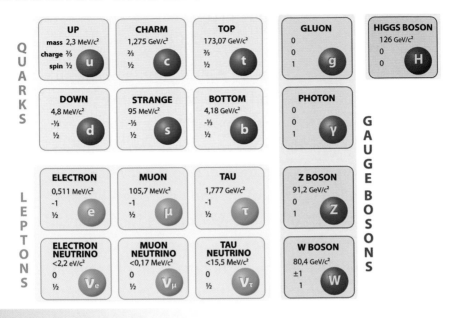

Up quarks. Down quarks. Gluons. Photons. Higgs boson. They're just a few of the elementary particles seen here.

particles. There are six types of leptons. The six leptons are the electron, the muon, the tau, the electron neutrino, the muon neutrino, and the tau neutrino. The muon forms an electron or positron when it decays. The tau has nearly four thousand times the mass of an electron. That is not the same as saying it is four thousand times as large as an electron. It's important to remember that the mass of a particle does not have anything to do with its size. The mass depends on the effect of the Higgs field on the particles in a substance. Even a small substance can have a large mass if it does not interact efficiently with the Higgs field.

Some other elementary particles are the gluon, the photon, the Z boson, the W boson, and the Higgs boson. Gluons bind quarks together. Photons are fundamental light particles. The recently discovered Higgs boson is thought to be an elementary particle. The Z and W bosons are elementary particles that are associated with atomic charges.

ANTIMATTER

Each type of particle—not just the elementary particles—has a corresponding antiparticle. This antimatter appears identical to its particle. The only difference is that the antimatter has an opposite charge. Think of it this way: if we know that up quarks have a positive charge, we also know that somewhere out there are anti-up quarks with a negative charge. When these particles meet, they annihilate one another. The result? Pure energy. The existence of antimatter leads to more questions. For instance, if there is an equal amount of matter and antimatter in the universe, why is there so much more matter visible in the universe? Scientists don't yet know, but they are working to discover the answer.

THE HIGGS FIELD AND THE HIGGS BOSON

What gives the matter in the universe its mass? When we push against a rock or car, or kick a soccer ball, what is the source of the resistance we encounter? We can say that the mass comes from the particles that make up the object. It can be due to the mass of the electrons and other fundamental particles. Where do those particles get their mass?

Peter Higgs, a British particle physicist, has wondered and theorized about the source of mass in the universe for more than fifty years. Using math, existing theories, and his understanding of the universe, he developed a theory that called for the universe to be filled with a Higgs field—a sort of viscous cosmic substance like molasses—that required particles to push their way through space. Higgs theorized that this effort to push was the basis for the resistance we feel. This resistance was, in turn, the source of mass.

Not all of this made sense because if particles did have to push, they would experience a sort of friction that would cause them to slow and stop. Higgs theorized this did not happen because the particles were subject to this resistance only when they tried to speed up or slow down. Also, the field would not affect all particles in the same way. Not all particles would affect other particles in the same way. Higgs theorized the one boson that would have an influence on all the others would be the ultimate elementary particle. He named this the Higgs boson. This particle would not spin like other particles, but it would be responsible for the mass of everything in the universe.

In March 2013, scientists confirmed that the boson discovered in the Large Hadron Collider in Geneva, Switzerland, in July 2012 was in fact a Higgs boson.

How Do We Know They're There?

Since these particles are very, very small, it's not as if we can easily see them. It's also the case that physicists theorize the existence of a particle before they can directly observe that particle. So how do we know the particles exist if we can't see them? We can tell from the way larger particles act.

Think about it this way: long before it was possible to view the planets and stars with powerful telescopes, humans used their observations of the skies to theorize about what might be up there. They created theories about what they could not see that were based on

what they could see. In this way, they "guessed" at the existence of unseen planets, black holes, and other phenomena that were proven later, when the required technology was developed. All of these are examples of work that was done in classical physics, a field of physics in which many things can be observed with the

This image shows traces of particle collisions in slow speed.

naked eye. The Higgs boson is a prime example of this same type of meticulous work on the subatomic scale. Its existence was theorized nearly fifty years before we had the technology to prove its existence.

Fitting It All Together

Physicists would like to have a theory that unifies everything. This theory would explain the workings at the observable and micro levels. It would explain the ways in which it is possible for matter to be in more than one state at a time. It would facilitate an understanding of the way all of the forms of matter and energy combine in one great whole to work in harmony as a universe. This understanding would facilitate the development of new forms of travel and communication. It would make it possible to use our resources in the most efficient way possible, at a level that we can only imagine today.

With a thorough understanding of the micro and macro worlds, it might be possible to clean up environmental damage through the use of nanotechnology while other properties of those particles were engaged in promoting restoration of habitat without any additional effort. The uses of the knowledge physicists are currently seeking may seem as if they have no part in your daily life, but in the same way that an understanding of classical physics made it possible to fly people in airplanes, rocket men into space, and cross the oceans safely, the information gained through an understanding of the particles that make up the matter surrounding us may lead us in other directions that are every bit as valuable.

WHAT WOULD YOU BUILD?

The next time you look at an object and think that it is small, just consider how small that really is. If an atom is so tiny that you cannot see it, imagine how tiny the particles must be to make up that atom. If the mass of an object is not an indicator of its size, imagine how much greater the interaction with the Higgs field must be for a particle that has a mass that is several thousand times larger than another particle of the same size. How might that be possible? And if you could do anything you wished with the building blocks of matter, if you were in the position to know what those building blocks were and to understand their properties, what is it you would choose to create?

Timeline

450 BCE Democritus puts forth a theory suggesting that everything is composed of atoms—particles that cannot be divided, have empty space between them, move constantly, and cannot be destroyed.

1661 CE Robert Boyle proposes that matter is made up of corpuscles—tiny pieces of matter that are independent of one another.

1798 Sir Benjamin Thompson discovers the foundation for thermodynamics by noticing that heat generated by an activity is proportional to the work—energy that is transferred through force to another object—being done.

1801 Thomas Young performs double-slit experiment, which proves that light is a wave.

1842 Sadi Carnot proposes the existence of a heat-energy cycle.

1858 Balfour Stewart learns that blackbodies radiate and absorb energy of the same wavelength.

1862 James Clerk Maxwell states that all electromagnetic waves are massless and travel at the speed of light.

1869 Dmitri Ivanovich Mendeleyev introduces the periodic table.

Late 1800s Rudolf Clausius introduces two laws of thermodynamics.

1886 Wilhelm Wien determines a law of blackbody radiation.

1887 Heinrich Hertz observes sparks being discharged during the detection of an electromagnetic wave.

1897 J.J. Thomson creates a model of the atom known as the plum pudding model.

1900 Max Planck determines that energy exists in the form of quanta—packets of energy that travel in set amounts.

1905 Albert Einstein uses the photoelectric effect to discover the photon.

1909 Ernest Rutherford proposes a model of the atom known as the planetary model.

1912 Ernest Solvay founds the International Solvay Institutes for Physics and Chemistry to solve pressing problems in physics and chemistry.

1913 Niels Bohr suggests the solar system model of the atom.

1918 Max Planck is awarded a Nobel Prize for Physics.

1921 Albert Einstein is awarded a Nobel Prize for Physics.

1924 Louis de Broglie presents a theory of electrons as waves, suggesting that all matter has wave properties.

1924–1927 Werner Heisenberg and Niels Bohr devise the Copenhagen interpretation.

1926 Erwin Schrödinger put forth the electron cloud model of the atom. Schrödinger's wave function formula becomes the basis for wave mechanics.

1927 Werner Heisenberg develops the uncertainty principle. The Fifth Solvay Conference brings together the greatest physicists in the world.

1931 Ernst Ruska and Max Knoll built the first transmission electron microscope (TEM).

1959 Richard Feynman presents his seminal talk, "There's Plenty of Room at the Bottom," at CalTech.

1964 Peter Higgs theorizes the Higgs boson.

2000 The U.S. National Nanotechnology Initiative is founded.

2012 The Higgs boson is discovered.

amplitude The height of a wave, measured from its midpoint.

blackbody An object that exists in theory only, a blackbody absorbs 100 percent of the radiation it generates.

cavity The hollow space inside an object, such as an oven or kiln.

classical physics Physics that was developed prior to the end of the nineteenth century; physics of the visible world.

collider A machine that is designed to promote the collision of particles.

constant An unchanging value in a mathematical formula.

ionization The process by which an atom or molecule acquires a charge through the gain or loss of an electron.

microscope An instrument used to examine objects or details that are too small to see unaided.

Nobel Prize An international prize that is awarded for extraordinary work in physics, chemistry, literature, economics, physiology or medicine, and the promotion of peace.

particle A small piece of something; a building block.

point An exact position that does not have a size; it is only a position.

probe A blunt instrument used to explore an object.

quantum physics Physics that has been developed since the 1900s; physics of the subatomic world.

radiation The way in which electromagnetic waves travel.

spectrum The group of colors that results when light is separated.

theoretical Speculative; not known but thought to be for good reason.

thought experiment A mental exercise that forces the thinker to imagine a scenario.

ultraviolet Light that is not seen by the naked eye.

wave A movement that radiates energy in all directions at one time.

American Association for the Advancement of
Science (AAAS)
1200 New York Avenue NW
Washington, DC 20001
(202) 326-6400
Website: http://www.aaas.org
The AAAS is an international organization created
to advance science for the benefit of all people.
Its site includes information about journals,
careers, educational programs, and news.

Canada Science and Technology Museum
1867 St. Laurent Boulevard
Ottawa, ON K1G 5A3
Canada
(613) 991-3044
Website: http://sciencetech.technomuses.ca
The Canada Science and Technology Museum website features information about summer camps,
professional days, the permanent collection, and
visiting programs.

Canadian Association of Physicists (CAP)
Suite 112, MacDonald Building
University of Ottawa
150 Louis Pasteur Priv.
Ottawa, ON K1N 6N5
Canada

(613) 562-5614

Website: http://www.cap.ca

The CAP supports physics research and education in Canada. Its website has information about activities, careers, certification, publications, and opportunities for students.

CERN

Route de Meyrin 385

1217 Meyrin, Switzerland

+41 22 767 84 84

Website: http://home.web.cern.ch

CERN, the European Organization for Nuclear Research, is home to the Large Hadron Collider (LHC) used to identify the Higgs boson. This site has information for students. It also has information about ongoing research.

Marvell Nanofabrication Laboratory

University of California, Berkeley

520 Sutardja Dai Hall MS 1754

Berkeley, CA 24720

(510) 809-8600

Website: http://nanolab.berkeley.edu

The Marvell Nanofabrication Lab at UC Berkeley is a center for nano research and fabrication. On this site, you'll find information about the micro and nano labs and their histories.

MIT-Bates Linear Accelerator Center
21 Manning Avenue
Middleton, MA 01949
(617) 253-9200
Website: http://mitbates.lns.mit.edu/bates/
    control/main
The Bates Linear Accelerator Center has been a
    center for nuclear physics research for more than
    thirty years. You can learn more about the history
    of this research on this site.

National Science Foundation (NSF)
4201 Wilson Boulevard
Arlington, VA 22230
(800) 877-8339
Website: http://www.nsf.gov
The NSF is an independent federal agency
    tasked "to promote the progress of science."
    It is the only federal agency with a mission
    to support all fields of fundamental science
    and engineering.

Smithsonian National Air and Space Museum
Independence Avenue at 6th Street SW
Washington, DC 20560
(202) 633-2214
Website: http://www.airandspace.si.edu
The National Air and Space Museum has thousands

of objects on display. It also has an IMAX theater and planetarium. Its website includes information about events, exhibitions, collections, research, and educational opportunities.

Society of Physics Students (SPS)
American Institute of Physics
One Physics Ellipse
College Park, MD 20740
(301) 209-3007
Website: http://www.spsnational.org
The SPS is a professional association for students. Collegiate chapters offer membership to anyone interested in physics. Its purpose is to help students gain the knowledge and experience they require in order to become contributing members of the professional community.

Websites

Because of the changing nature of Internet links, Rosen Publishing has developed an online list of websites related to the subject of this book. This site is updated regularly. Please use this link to access the list:

http://www.rosenlinks.com/PHYS/Quan

Al-Khalil, Jim. *Paradox: The Nine Greatest Enigmas in Physics*. New York, NY: Broadway, 2012.

Brewster, David. *Memoirs of the Life, Writings, and Discoveries of Sir Isaac Newton*. Hamburg, Germany: Severus-Verl., 2013.

Carroll, Sean M. *The Particle at the End of the Universe: How the Hunt for the Higgs Boson Leads Us to the Edge of a New World*. New York, NY: Dutton, 2012.

Close, F. E. *The Infinity Puzzle: Quantum Field Theory and the Hunt for an Orderly Universe*. New York, NY: Basic Books, 2011.

Cox, Brian, and J. R. Forshaw. *The Quantum Universe (and Why Anything That Can Happen, Does)*. Boston, MA: Da Capo Press, 2012.

Crowther, J. G., and Patrick Cullen. *Six Great Scientists: Copernicus, Galileo, Newton, Darwin, Marie Curie, Einstein*. Ashland, OR: Blackstone Audio, 2013.

Foer, Joshua. *Moonwalking with Einstein: The Art and Science of Remembering Everything*. New York, NY: Penguin Press, 2011.

Fortey, Jacqueline. *Great Scientists*. London, England: DK, 2013.

Frenkel, Edward. *Love and Math: The Heart of Hidden Reality*. New York, NY: Basic Books, 2013.

Johnson, Rebecca L. *Atomic Structure*. Minneapolis, MN: Twenty-First Century Books, 2008.

Kuper, Tonya. *Anomaly*. Entangled Teen, 2014.

Le Bellac, Michel. *The Quantum World*. Hackensack, NJ: World Scientific, 2014.

Lee, John V. *Search for the Higgs Boson*. New York, NY: Nova Science Publishers, 2006.

Lindenfeld, Peter, and Suzanne White Brahmia. *Physics: The First Science*. New Brunswick, NJ: Rutgers University Press, 2011.

Moffat, John W. *Cracking the Particle Code of the Universe: The Hunt for the Higgs Boson*. Oxford, England: Oxford University Press, 2014.

Muir, Hazel. *Science in Seconds: 200 Key Concepts Explained in an Instant*. New York, NY: Quercus, 2013.

Muller, R. *Physics for Future Presidents: The Science Behind the Headlines*. New York, NY: W. W. Norton & Co., 2008.

Pohlen, Jerome. *Albert Einstein and Relativity for Kids: His Life and Ideas with 21 Activities and Thought Experiments*. Chicago, IL: Chicago Review Press, 2012.

Schwartz, Matthew Dean. *Quantum Field Theory and the Standard Model*. New York, NY: Cambridge University Press, 2014.

St. John, Allen, and Ainissa Ramírez. *Newton's Football: The Science Behind America's Game*. New York, NY: Ballantine Books, 2013.

Susskind, Leonard, and Art Friedman. *The Theoretical Minimum: Quantum Mechanics*. New York, NY: Basic Books, 2014.

Tangey, Penny. *Loving Richard Feynman*. Chicago, IL: University of Queensland Press, 2009.

Wolke, Robert L., Sean Runnette, and Marlene Parrish. *What Einstein Told His Cook: Kitchen Science Explained*. Old Saybrook, CT: Tantor Media, 2012.

Yuki, Hiroshi, and Tony Gonzales. *Math Girls*. Austin, TX: Bento Books, 2011.

Yuki, Hiroshi, Tony Gonzalez, and Joseph Reeder. *Math Girls^2: Fermat's Last Theorem*. Austin, TX: Bento Books, 2012.

Zitzewitz, Paul W. *The Handy Physics Answer Book*. Detroit, MI: Visible Ink Press, 2011.

Al-Khalili, Jim. *Quantum: A Guide for the Perplexed.*
London, England: Weidenfeld & Nicolson, 2004.

Baggott, J. E. *The Quantum Story: A History in 40 Movements.* Oxford, England: Oxford University Press, 2011.

Bloomfield, Louis. *How Things Work: The Physics of Everyday Life.* Hoboken, NJ: Wiley, 2010.

Clegg, Brian. *The Universe Inside You: The Extreme Science of the Human Body from Quantum Theory to the Mysteries of the Brain.* London, England: Icon Books, 2012.

Encyclopædia Britannica Online. "Quantum Mechanics." Retrieved February 08, 2014 (http://www.britannica.com/EBchecked/topic/486231/quantum-mechanics).

Fayer, Michael D. *Absolutely Small: How Quantum Theory Explains Our Everyday World.* New York, NY: AMACOM, 2010.

Fernandez-Armesto, Felipe. *Ideas That Changed the World.* New York, NY: Dorling Kindersley, 2003.

Ford, Kenneth William. *101 Quantum Questions: What You Need to Know About the World You Can't See.* Cambridge, MA: Harvard University Press, 2011.

Krauss, Lawrence Maxwekk, and Cormac McCarthy. *Quantum Man: Richard Feynman's Life in Science.* New York, NY: W. W. Norton, 2012.

Kumar, Manjit. *Quantum: Einstein, Bohr, and the*

Great Debate About the Nature of Reality. New York, NY: W. W. Norton, 2011.

Liboff, Richard. *Introductory Quantum Mechanics.* San Francisco, CA: Addison-Wesley, 2003.

"Max Planck and Quantum Physics." April 28, 2013. Video. Retrieved February 7, 2014 (https://www.youtube.com/watch?v=DniOX8G-BeE).

McEvoy, J. P., and Oscar Zarate. *Introducing Quantum Theory: A Graphic Guide.* Tarxien, Malta: Gutenberg Press, 2009.

"Michio Kaku–Quantum Mechanics vs. General Relativity." April 2, 2013. Video. Retrieved February 5, 2014 (https://www.youtube.com/watch?v=t2mjoI7bgXM).

Oswego City School District. "Regents Exam Prep Center Physics–The Bohr Model." Retrieved January 27, 2014 (http://www.regentsprep.org/Regents/physics/phys05/catomodel/ruther.htm).

Oswego City School District. "Regents Exam Prep Center Physics–The Cloud Model." Retrieved January 27, 2014 (http://www.regentsprep.org/Regents/physics/phys05/catomodel/cloud.htm).

Oswego City School District. "Regents Exam Prep Center Physics–The Rutherford Model." Retrieved January 27, 2014 (http://www.regentsprep.org/Regents/physics/phys05/catomodel/bohr.htm).

Pickover, Clifford A. *The Physics Book: From the Big Bang to Quantum Resurrection: 250 Milestones in the History of Physics.* New York, NY: Sterling Publishing, 2011.

Spielberg, Nathan, and Bryon D. Anderson. *Seven Ideas That Shook the Universe.* Hoboken, NJ: Wiley, 1987.

Susskind, Leonard, and George Hrabovsky. *The Theoretical Minimum: What You Need to Know to Start Doing Physics.* New York, NY: Basic Books, 2013.

ABOUT THE AUTHOR

Gina Hagler writes about science and technology for children and adults. Her science experiment books for kids cover topics ranging from magnets to simple machines. She also has a KidSci section on her blog.

PHOTO CREDITS

Cover © iSockphoto.com/agsandrew; p. 4 Universal Images Group/Getty Images; pp. 6, 34, 51, 58–59, 62–63 Science & Society Picture Library/Getty Images; p. 9 Photos.com/Thinkstock; p. 13 Claus Andersen/Getty Images; pp. 14–15 Phil Degginger/Science Source; p. 19 Friedrich Saurer/Science Source; p. 23 John Burke/Photolibrary/Getty Images; pp. 24–25 Dave King/Dorling Kindersley/Getty Images; p. 27 Science Source; p. 38 Wolfmankurd/Wikimedia Commons/File:Photoelectric effect.svg/CC BY 3.0; p. 42 SPL/Science Source; p. 45 DEA/Pedicini/De Agostini/Getty Images; p. 47 Iaryna Turchyniak/Shutterstock.com; pp. 52, 61 Encyclopaedia Britannica/Getty Images; p. 54 Keystone/Hulton Archive/Getty Images; pp. 70–71 Medi-Mation/Science Photo Library/Getty Images; pp. 74–75 Cynthia Goldsmith/CDC; pp. 76–77 Stegerphoto/Photolibrary/Getty Images; p. 80 Victor Habbick Visions/Science Source; p. 84 Designua/Shutterstock.com; pp. 88–89 Fabrice Coffrini/AFP/Getty Images; cover and interior design elements Shutterstock.com.

Designer: Les Kanturek ; Editor: Christine Poolos;
Photo Researcher: Cindy Reiman